cookies

cookies

RYLAND
PETERS
& SMALL

LONDON NEW YORK

Designer Sally Powell

Commissioning Editor
Julia Charles

Picture Research
Emily Westlake

Production Eleanor Cant

Art Director Anne-Marie Bulat

Publishing Director
Alison Starling

Index Hilary Bird

Notes
All spoon measurements
are level unless otherwise
specified. If you are using
a fan-assisted oven, adjust
cooking times according to
the manufacturer's instructions.

First published in the
United States in 2006
by Ryland Peters & Small, Inc.
519 Broadway, 5th Floor
New York, NY 10012
www.rylandpeters.com

10 9 8 7 6 5 4 3 2

Text copyright ©
Linda Collister, Clare Ferguson,
Liz Franklin, Louise Pickford,
Fran Warde, Ryland Peters &
Small, 2006

Design and photographs
copyright ©
Ryland Peters & Small, 2006

ISBN-13: 978 1 84597 291 2
ISBN-10: 1 84597 291 0

Library of Congress Cataloging-
in-Publication Data is available
on request.

Printed in China

contents

introduction

Who can resist a homemade cookie still warm from the oven? Add a good cup of coffee, tea, or glass of chilled milk and settle down to enjoy a moment of pure pleasure. Here you will find perfect cookie recipes for every occasion. Whether you want to enjoy a little luxury every day, spoil yourself with an occasional self-indulgent treat or surprise a friend with a thoughtful gift, these simple, no-fuss recipes make it easy. You will need to use the very best ingredients to get the best cookies so buy the highest quality you can find and you'll really appreciate the results. But be warned, you may never want to eat a store-bought cookie again once you've baked your own!

cookie jar classics

These cookies are always popular, whether plain or flavored with dried fruit. Use old-fashioned oatmeal or rolled oats rather than "instant."

classic oat cookies

1 stick unsalted butter, very soft

¾ cup firmly packed light brown sugar

1 extra-large egg, beaten

1 tablespoon milk

½ teaspoon real vanilla extract

¾ cup plus 1 tablespoon self-rising flour

½ cup dried fruit such as raisins, cherries, cranberries, or blueberries (optional)

1½ cups coarse oatmeal or rolled oats

2 cookie sheets, very lightly greased

makes about 24

Put the butter, sugar, egg, milk, and vanilla in a bowl and beat well using an electric mixer, or a wooden spoon. Add the flour, dried fruit (if using) and oats and mix well with the wooden spoon.

Put heaped teaspoons of dough onto the prepared cookie sheets, spacing them well apart.

Bake in a preheated oven at 350°F for 12–15 minutes until lightly browned around the edges.

Let cool on the sheets for 2 minutes, then transfer to a wire rack to cool completely.

Store in an airtight container and eat within 5 days or freeze for up to a month.

For the best flavor, use an all-natural peanut butter with no added sugar or fat. The crunchy coating is made by rolling the cookie mixture in roasted (but unsalted) peanuts before baking.

extra-crunchy peanut butter cookies

1 stick unsalted butter, softened

½ cup crunchy peanut butter

¾ cup firmly packed light brown sugar

1 extra-large egg, lightly beaten

½ teaspoon real vanilla extract

1½ cups self-rising flour

1½ cups roasted unsalted peanut halves

2 cookie sheets, greased

makes about 20

Put the butter, peanut butter, sugar, beaten egg, vanilla extract, and flour in a large bowl. Mix well with a wooden spoon. When thoroughly combined, take walnut-sized portions of the dough (about a tablespoon) and roll into balls with your hands. Put the peanut halves in a shallow dish, then roll the dough in the nuts. Arrange the balls well apart on the prepared sheets, then gently flatten slightly with your fingers.

Bake in a preheated oven at 350°F for 12–15 minutes until light golden brown.

Let cool on the sheets for a couple of minutes to firm up, then transfer to a wire rack to cool completely.

Store in an airtight container and eat within 5 days or freeze for up to a month.

For a spicier Candied Ginger Cookie simply replace the molasses with light corn syrup, finely chop 2 pieces of candied ginger and add with the egg.

gingerbread cookies

1⅓ cup self-rising flour

a pinch of salt

1 cup superfine of granulated sugar, plus extra for sprinkling

2 teaspoons ground ginger

2 teaspoons ground cinnamon

1 teaspoon baking soda

1 stick unsalted butter

¼ cup molasses

1 extra-large egg, beaten

2 cookie sheets, lightly greased

makes about 30

Sift the flour, salt, sugar, ginger, cinnamon, and baking soda into a large bowl. Heat the butter and molasses very gently in a small saucepan until melted. Pour onto the dry ingredients, add the beaten egg, and mix thoroughly with a wooden spoon.

Using your hands, roll the dough into 30 walnut-sized balls. Arrange well apart on the prepared sheets, then flatten with your fingers. Sprinkle with a little sugar, then bake in a preheated oven at 325°F for 12–15 minutes or until firm and lightly browned.

Remove from the oven and let cool on the sheets for 2 minutes. Transfer to a wire rack to cool completely.

Store in an airtight container and eat within 5 days or freeze for up to a month.

Walnuts make wonderful cookies, but other nuts such as pecans or hazelnuts will also work just as well in this recipe.

walnut cookies

7 tablespoons unsalted butter, at room temperature

⅓ cup superfine or granulated sugar

⅓ cup raw or white sugar

1 large egg, beaten

½ teaspoon real vanilla extract

1⅔ cups self-rising flour

½ cup walnut pieces, chopped

2 cookie sheets, greased

makes about 24

Using a wooden spoon or electric mixer, beat the butter until soft and creamy. Gradually beat in the sugars and continue beating for another 2 minutes.

Beat in the egg a little at a time, then stir in the vanilla extract, flour, and nuts. Work the mixture with your hands until it comes together into a firm dough. Again using your hands, roll the dough into 24 walnut-sized balls.

Put the balls, spaced well apart, on the prepared sheets, then flatten with a fork. Bake in a preheated oven at 350°F for about 10 minutes, until golden and firm.

Remove from the oven, leave on the cookie sheets for a couple of minutes to firm up, then transfer to a wire rack to cool completely.

Store in an airtight container and eat within 1 week, or freeze for up to a month.

Always popular and hard to beat! This classic recipe has been adapted so that it uses less sugar and more nuts. Use semisweet chocolate broken up into chunks or a bag of good quality chocolate chips.

classic choc chip cookies

1⅓ cups self-rising flour

a pinch of salt

a good pinch of baking soda

1 stick unsalted butter, very soft

⅓ cup minus 1 tablespoon superfine sugar

⅓ cup lightly packed light brown sugar

½ teaspoon real vanilla extract

1 extra-large egg, lightly beaten

1 cup semisweet chocolate broken into chunks or chocolate chips

¾ cup walnut or pecan pieces

2 cookie sheets, greased

makes about 24

Put all the ingredients in a large bowl and mix thoroughly with a wooden spoon.

Drop heaped teaspoons of the mixture onto the prepared sheets, spacing them well apart.

Bake in a preheated oven at 375°F for 8–10 minutes until lightly colored and just firm.

Let cool on the sheets for a minute, then transfer to a wire rack to cool completely.

Store in an airtight container and eat within 5 days or freeze for up to a month.

Parkin is a kind of sticky gingerbread from Yorkshire, England, made with oatmeal, molasses, and spice. These cookies are made from the same ingredients and have the same flavor and a crunchy texture.

parkin cookies

¾ cup plus 2 tablespoons self-rising flour

¾ cup fine oatmeal

1 teaspoon ground ginger

½ teaspoon ground allspice

3 tablespoons dark brown sugar

6 tablespoons unsalted butter

2 tablespoons light corn syrup

1 tablespoon molasses

confectioners' sugar, for dusting (optional)

2 cookie sheets, greased

makes about 20

Put the flour, oatmeal, ginger, allspice, and sugar in a large bowl and mix well. Make a hollow in the centre.

Put the butter, light corn syrup, and molasses in a small saucepan and heat gently until melted. Pour the mixture into the hollow in the dry ingredients and mix well with a wooden spoon.

Using floured hands, take walnut-sized portions of the dough (about a tablespoon) and roll into balls. Set well apart on the prepared sheets. Bake in a preheated oven at 350°F for about 15 minutes or until firm.

Let cool on the cookie sheets for 2 minutes to firm up, then transfer to a wire rack to cool completely. Serve dusted with confectioners' sugar, if using.

Store in an airtight container and eat within 5 days or freeze for up to a month.

heavenly chocolate

Make chocolate chips by chopping a bar of good bittersweet chocolate into large chunks—the flavor is far superior to commercial chocolate chips.

black and white cookies

1 stick unsalted butter, at room temperature

scant ½ cup light brown sugar

1 large egg, beaten

scant ½ cup self-rising flour

½ teaspoon baking powder

a pinch of salt

½ teaspoon real vanilla extract

1½ cups rolled oats (not instant)

6½ oz. bittersweet chocolate, chopped into chunks

2 cookie sheets, greased

makes about 24

Using a wooden spoon or electric beater, cream the butter until smooth and creamy. Add the sugar and beat until light and fluffy. Gradually beat in the egg, beating well after the last addition. Sift the flour, baking powder, and salt into the mixture, add the vanilla extract and rolled oats and stir in. When thoroughly mixed, stir in the chocolate chunks.

Put heaped teaspoons of the cookie mixture, spaced well apart, on the prepared sheets. Bake in a preheated oven at 350°F for 12–15 minutes until golden and just firm. Remove from the oven and let cool on the sheets for a couple of minutes until firm enough to transfer to a wire rack to cool completely.

Store in an airtight container. Eat within 1 week, or freeze for up to a month.

Good quality semisweet chocolate is used in these cookies both as chunks and as a powder (by simply processing it with the flour.)

double chocolate pecans

1 cup old-fashioned oatmeal or rolled oats (not instant)

1¼ cups all-purpose flour

½ teaspoon baking powder

½ teaspoon baking soda

½ cup firmly packed light brown sugar

7 oz. semisweet chocolate, broken up

1 stick unsalted butter, very soft

1 extra-large egg, beaten

1 cup pecan pieces

2 cookie sheets, greased

makes 24

Put the oats in a food processor. Add the flour, baking powder, baking soda, the sugar, and half of the chocolate pieces. Process until the mixture has a sandy texture.

Put the soft butter, beaten egg, pecan pieces, and the remaining pieces of chocolate in a large bowl. Add the mixture from the processor and mix well with a wooden spoon or your hands to make a firm dough.

Roll walnut-sized pieces of dough into balls using your hands. Arrange well apart on the prepared sheets and flatten slightly with the back of a fork. Bake in a preheated oven at 375°F for 12–15 minutes until almost firm.

Let cool on the sheets for 2 minutes, then transfer to a wire rack to cool completely.

Store in an airtight container and eat within 5 days or freeze for up to a month.

A very quick, rich recipe using chocolate and a food processor. These cookies are particularly good served with vanilla ice cream.

chocolate fudge cookies

⅓ cup superfine sugar

½ cup firmly packed light brown sugar

5 oz. good semisweet chocolate, broken up

1 stick unsalted butter, chilled and cut into small pieces

1¼ cups all-purpose flour

½ teaspoon baking powder

1 extra-large egg, lightly beaten

2 cookie sheets, greased

makes about 20

Put both the sugars in a food processor. Add the chocolate, then process until the mixture has a sandy texture.

Add the pieces of butter, flour, baking powder, and egg and process until the mixture comes together to make a firm dough. Carefully remove from the machine.

Lightly flour your hands and roll the dough into about 20 walnut-sized balls. Arrange them, spaced well apart, on the prepared sheets. Bake in a preheated oven at 350°F for 12–15 minutes until firm.

Let cool on the sheets for 2 minutes, then transfer to wire racks to cool completely.

Store in an airtight container and eat within 5 days or freeze for up to a month.

These dark, dark chocolate cookies have a white "crazy-paving" top. The effect is created by rolling the cookies in confectioners' sugar just before baking. The surface then cracks to form the "paving."

chocolate crackle cookies

3½ oz. semisweet chocolate, broken up

1 stick unsalted butter, cut into small pieces

1 cup firmly packed light brown sugar

1 extra-large egg, beaten

2–3 drops real vanilla extract

1⅓ cups self-rising flour

½ teaspoon baking soda

2 tablespoons confectioners' sugar

2 cookie sheets, greased

makes about 24

Put the chocolate, butter, and sugar in a heatproof bowl and set over a saucepan of gently steaming water. Melt gently, stirring occasionally until smooth.

Remove the bowl from the pan and let cool for a minute. Stir in the egg, vanilla, flour, and baking soda. Mix well. Cover the bowl and chill until firm, about 20 minutes.

Put the confectioners' sugar in a shallow dish. Using your hands, roll the dough into walnut-sized balls, then roll in the confectioners' sugar to coat thoroughly. Set the balls on the prepared sheets, spacing them well apart. Bake in a preheated oven at 400°F for 10–12 minutes until just set.

Let cool on the sheet for 2 minutes, then transfer to a wire rack to cool completely.

Store in an airtight container and eat within 5 days or freeze for up to a month.

Only the very finest unsweetened chocolate is suitable for this sophisticated and delicious cookie.

bitter chocolate
butter cookies

2½ oz. unsweetened chocolate, roughly chopped

1½ tablespoons superfine or granulated sugar

2 sticks unsalted butter, chilled and cut into pieces

¾ cup light brown sugar

1⅔ cups all-purpose flour

½ teaspoon real vanilla extract

2 oz. white or unsweetened chocolate, melted, to decorate

2 cookie sheets, well greased

makes about 30

Put the chopped chocolate and superfine sugar in a food processor and process until they form the texture of sand. Add the butter, sugar, flour, and vanilla extract, then process again just until the dough comes together.

Using your hands, form the dough into about 30 walnut-sized balls. Arrange them on the prepared cookie sheets, spacing them well apart.

Bake the cookies in a preheated oven at 350°F for 10–15 minutes or until they are just firm to the touch and beginning to color around the edges.

Remove from the oven. Leave them for 5 minutes to firm up before transferring to a wire rack to cool. When they are cold, decorate by drizzling with the melted chocolate.

Store in an airtight container and eat within 4 days. Undecorated cookies can be frozen for up to a month.

These delicious macaroons have a crisp outside and are soft and chewy inside but it is the creamy white chocolate filling that makes them extra special.

double chocolate macaroons

3 oz. bittersweet chocolate, chopped

2 large egg whites, at room temperature

1 cup superfine sugar

1 cup firmly packed slivered almonds, finely ground in a food processor

2–3 drops almond extract

4 oz. white chocolate, chopped

½ cup heavy cream

2 cookie sheets, lined with nonstick parchment paper

makes about 8

Put the bittersweet chocolate into a heatproof bowl set over a pan of steaming water and melt. Remove the bowl from the heat and stir until smooth. Set aside. Put the egg whites into a bowl and whisk until stiff peaks form. Gradually whisk in the sugar to make a thick, glossy meringue. Fold in the almonds, almond extract, and melted chocolate. When blended, put a tablespoonful of the mixture at a time onto the cookie sheets and spread to make 2-inch discs.

Bake in a preheated oven at 300°F for 30 minutes until just firm. Remove from the oven and let cool on the trays. When cold, gently peel away from the parchment paper.

Put the white chocolate and cream into a small saucepan and heat very gently, until melted and smooth. Remove from the heat, let cool, then beat until thick and fluffy. Use it to sandwich the cold macaroons together.

Store in an airtight container. Best eaten within 5 days.

A few drops of Tabasco gives these moist and rich cookies a fascinating, subtle flavor. Ask your friends if they can guess the mystery ingredient!

macadamia and white choc chile cookies

1¼ cups macadamia nuts

1⅔ cups all-purpose flour

½ teaspoon baking powder

⅔ cup firmly packed light brown sugar

1 stick unsalted butter, very soft

1 extra-large egg, lightly beaten

5 drops Tabasco

3½ oz. white chocolate, broken into chunks, or chips

2 cookie sheets, lightly greased

makes about 20

Put the nuts in an ovenproof dish and toast in a preheated oven at 350°F for 5–7 minutes until light golden brown. Let cool, then chop coarsely by hand or in a food processor. Leave the oven on.

Put the chopped nuts, flour, baking powder, sugar, butter, egg, Tabasco, and chocolate pieces in a large bowl and mix thoroughly with a wooden spoon.

Using about a tablespoon of the mixture for each cookie, drop each spoonful onto the prepared cookie sheets, spacing well apart. Bake in the heated oven for 12–15 minutes until light golden brown.

Let cool on the sheets for 2 minutes, then transfer to a wire rack to cool completely.

Store in an airtight container and eat within 4 days or freeze for up to a month.

occasional treats

Pecans are the most popular nuts in North America, and were particularly prized by Algonquin Indians, who gave them their name paccan. In the South, they are used to enrich stuffings, breads, cakes, and cookies, as well as baked in pies. These rich and crumbly cookies are found in New Mexico.

santa fe wedding cookies

1 cup all-purpose flour

¼ cup light brown sugar

7 tablespoons unsalted butter, very soft

½ teaspoon real vanilla extract

½ cup pecan pieces, coarsely chopped

20 pecan halves, to decorate

confectioners' sugar, to dust

2 cookie sheets, greased

makes about 20

Put the flour, sugar, soft butter, vanilla, and pecans in a bowl. Using a wooden spoon, work the ingredients until they come together to form a soft dough.

Using your hands, lightly floured, roll the mixture into about 20 walnut-sized balls. Arrange them slightly apart on the prepared cookie sheets, then gently press a pecan half on top of each cookie. Bake in a preheated oven at 350°F for 10–12 minutes until a light golden colour with slightly brown edges.

Remove from the oven, let cool on the cookie sheets for 2 minutes, then transfer to a wire rack to cool completely. Dust with plenty of confectioners' sugar before serving. Handle carefully as these cookies are fragile.

Store in an airtight container and eat within 5 days, or freeze for up to a month.

These sweet, almond-rich cookies are like soft, chewy amaretti. Serve with coffee at the end a special meal or give a box of them as a gift.

sardinian wedding cookies

¾ cup (1 lb.) almond paste

⅔ cup slivered almonds, plus an extra ⅓ cup for sprinkling

2 large egg whites

1 scant ½ cup confectioners' sugar

2 cookie sheets, lined with nonstick parchment paper

makes about 30

Break up the almond paste and put in a food processor. Process briefly until the paste is finely chopped. Add the almonds, egg whites, and sugar and process until the mixture forms a thick, smooth paste.

Using a tablespoon of mixture for each cookie, drop or spoon the mixture onto the prepared cookie sheets, spacing the cookies slightly apart. Scatter the remaining almonds over the top of the cookies.

Bake in a preheated oven at 300°F for about 25 minutes until light golden brown. Let cool completely on the sheets, then remove the cookies.

Store in an airtight container and eat within a week. These cookies don't freeze very well.

These cookies are made with the same ingredients used for a traditional British Christmas cake. Use mixed dried fruit or the "luxury" type, which includes cherries, and a mix of nuts such as Brazils, walnuts, almonds, and hazelnuts.

christmas cake cookies

1²/₃ cups self-rising flour

¹/₈ teaspoon grated nutmeg

¹/₂ teaspoon apple pie spice

²/₃ cup firmly packed dark brown sugar

1 stick unsalted butter, chilled and cut into pieces

2 large eggs, beaten

2 tablespoons sweet sherry, brandy or milk

1 cup chopped mixed nuts

1 cup mixed dried fruit (such as raisins, golden raisins, and currants)

soft brown sugar, for sprinkling

2 cookie sheets, greased

makes about 20

Sieve the flour, nutmeg, and apple pie spice into a large bowl. Stir in the sugar. Add the pieces of butter and rub into the flour using the tips of your fingers until the mixture looks like coarse crumbs. You can also cut the butter into the flour using a knife or special pastry cutter. Add the eggs, sherry (or brandy or milk if using), nuts, and dried fruit to the bowl and mix thoroughly with a wooden spoon.

Drop tablespoons of the mixture onto the prepared sheets, spacing them well apart. Flatten them slightly with the back of a fork and sprinkle lightly with soft brown sugar.

Bake in a preheated oven at 350°F for 12–15 minutes, until golden brown. Let cool on the sheets for 2 minutes to firm up, then transfer to a cooling rack to cool completely.

Store in an airtight container and eat within 5 days, or freeze for up to a month.

These fragrant, crumbly *kourambiedes* are served all year round, but especially at Christmas, usually with syrupy fruit and nut preserves, known as *glyka*.

greek shortbread cookies

1 stick plus 6 tablespoons butter, at room temperature

½ cup plus 1 tablespoon sugar

2 egg yolks

1 teaspoon real vanilla extract

2 tablespoons brandy or Cognac

20 green cardamom pods, crushed, black seeds extracted

½ cup flaked almonds, chopped or crushed

1 teaspoon baking powder

2⅔ cups all-purpose flour

To finish:

2 tablespoons rose water

2 tablespoons brandy or Cognac

1½ cups confectioners' sugar

2 cookie sheets, greased

makes about 34

Put the butter and sugar in a bowl and beat until light and pale. Beat in the egg yolks, vanilla, brandy, cardamom, and almonds. Add the baking powder and two-thirds of the flour and stir to form a soft, sticky dough. Stir in enough of the remaining flour to make a soft, manageable dough.

Take 1 heaped tablespoon of dough, put it on a floured counter and roll it into an oval. Set it on one of the prepared cookie sheets, then push and pinch the ends into a half-moon shape. Repeat this process to make 34 pieces.

Bake in a preheated oven at 325°F for 20–22 minutes or until pale, golden and firm, then remove and let cool on wire racks.

Mix the rose water and brandy in a bowl. Put the sifted confectioners' sugar in another. Partially dip each cookie in the flavoring, then dip it into the sugar until thickly coated.

Store in layers in a wax paper lined container until ready to serve. Best eaten within 5 days.

These tasty cookies can be made into pretty holiday decorations by cutting the dough into tree, star, or bell shapes, and threading with ribbons for hanging.

german honey spice cookies

1¼ cups all-purpose flour

1 teaspoon ground cinnamon

¼ teaspoon ground ginger

¼ teaspoon apple pie spice

6 tablespoons unsalted butter, chilled and cut into small pieces

3 tablespoons honey

To finish (optional):

thin ribbon for hanging, edible frosting writing pens and silver balls

shaped cookie cutters

2 cookie sheets, greased

makes about 12

Put the flour, cinnamon, ginger, and apple pie spice in a food processor. Add the butter and blend until the mixture looks like crumbs. Add the honey and process until it forms a soft dough. Remove the dough from the processor, wrap in plastic wrap or wax paper, and chill for 30 minutes.

Lightly flour the counter and a rolling pin, then roll out the dough to about ¼ inch thick. Cut out shapes using cookie cutters. Use a toothpick to pierce a hole at the top of each one, large enough to thread a thin ribbon through.

Arrange the shapes on the prepared sheets and chill for 10 minutes. Bake in a preheated oven at 350°F for about 10 minutes until golden. Leave for 5 minutes, then transfer to a wire rack to cool. Decorate when cold.

Best eaten within 24 hours, or store in an airtight container and eat within 4 days. Undecorated cookies can be frozen for up to a month.

little indulgences

These "kisses" are delicate little walnut and coffee cookies joined with a rich chocolate-coffee ganache—a real treat!

walnut coffee kisses

1 stick unsalted butter

4½ tablespoons superfine sugar

½ large beaten egg

¾ cup self-rising flour

1 teaspoon instant espresso powder

⅓ cup walnut halves, finely chopped

For the ganache:

4 oz. bittersweet chocolate

4 tablespoons unsalted butter

½ cup heavy cream

1½ teaspoons instant espresso powder

2 cookie sheets, lined with nonstick parchment paper

makes about 12

Put the butter and sugar into a bowl and beat until creamy. Stir in the beaten egg and then fold in the sifted flour. Stir in the espresso powder, then the walnuts.

Put an even number (about 24) tablespoons of the mixture onto cookie sheets covered with non-stick parchment. Bake in a preheated oven at 350°F for about 10 minutes or until light-brown around the edges. Remove from the oven and let cool and firm up on the sheet for a couple of minutes, then carefully transfer to a wire rack to cool completely.

Meanwhile, to make the ganache, break the chocolate into pieces and put into a small saucepan. Heat with butter and cream without boiling, until the butter melts. Beat in the espresso powder. Remove from the heat and stir. The mixture will thicken as it cools. Carefully sandwich the cool cookies together with the ganache.

Store in an airtight container and eat within 24 hours.

What a combination! The two most popular sweet things sandwiched together. If you really do run out of time and can't make the cookies yourself then by all means buy them, but they will not be as good as this recipe!

chocolate chip cookie ice cream cakes

3½ sticks of unsalted butter

1¾ cups plus 2 tablespoons superfine sugar

3 large eggs

1 teaspoon real vanilla extract

2½ cups all-purpose flour

13 oz. (about 13 squares) bittersweet chocolate, chopped

2½ quarts good ice cream

2 cookie sheets, lined with nonstick parchment paper

makes about 24

Put the butter and sugar into a bowl and beat until light and fluffy. Add the eggs and vanilla and beat well. Add the flour and chocolate and fold until smooth. Working in batches, spoon out 48 portions of the mixture (2 teaspoons each) onto the prepared cookie sheets, making sure each cookie has enough room to spread (they will triple in size!). Bake in the middle of a preheated oven at 350°F for about 15 minutes until lightly golden. Remove from the oven and let cool on the cookie sheets for 5 minutes. Transfer to a wire cooling rack and let cool completely.

Sandwich 2 cookies together with ice cream, arrange on a tray, cover well with foil, and return to the freezer until needed. Transfer to the refrigerator 20–30 minutes before serving so that the ice cream can soften a little.

This is one for the kids, and one for the adults who remember grilling these deliciously gooey treats over a campfire when they were young. Although traditionally made with whole-wheat graham crackers you can use sweet cookies, such as *langue du chat* or almond thins—they will work just as well.

s'mores

16 cookies of your choice (either homemade or store bought)

8 squares of semisweet chocolate

16 marshmallows

8 metal skewers

a barbecue

makes 4

Put 8 of the cookies onto a plate and top each one with a square of chocolate.

Preheat the barbecue. Thread 2 marshmallows onto each skewer and cook over hot coals for about 2 minutes, turning constantly until the marshmallows are melted and blackened. Remove from the heat and let cool slightly.

Put the marshmallows on top of the chocolate squares and sandwich together with the remaining cookies.

Gently ease out the skewers and eat the s'mores as soon as the chocolate melts.

Though Austrian bakers are credited with inventing these cookies, their name implies an Italian heritage. The chewy, candylike florentine has a flat side which is coated with chocolate, then combed to give an attactive wavy pattern or feathered (dragged) design.

tiny florentines

6 tablespoons unsalted butter

3½ tablespoons light corn syrup

3 tablespoons all-purpose flour

scant ½ cup chopped almonds

3 tablespoons chopped dried candied citrus peel

scant ½ cup golden raisins or candied fruit

½ cup candied cherries, chopped

4 oz. chocolate—bittersweet or white—or some of each, melted

2 cookie sheets, lined with nonstick parchment paper

makes about 20

Put the butter and syrup into a medium, heavy-based saucepan and heat until melted. Stir in all the remaining ingredients except the chocolate.

Put teaspoonfuls of the mixture onto the prepared cookie sheets, spacing them well apart. Flatten lightly, then bake in a preheated oven at 350°F for 7–8 minutes until light golden brown. Remove from the oven and let cool for 1–2 minutes or until firm enough to transfer to a wire rack to cool completely.

When cool, coat the flat underside of each florentine with the melted chocolate and, using a serrated frosting spatula or small fork, make a wavy pattern in the chocolate. Leave to set, chocolate side up.

Store in a cool place in an airtight container. Best eaten within a week.

Use good-quality cookies, made with butter if possible—and of course, plenty of real chocolate chips. Inferior cookies will spoil the ice cream by giving it a greasy aftertaste when frozen.

chocolate chip cookie ice cream

8 oz. mascarpone cheese

1 cup whole milk

½ cup firmly packed light brown sugar

6 oz. chocolate chip cookies, crumbled

an ice cream machine (optional)

makes about 4–6 servings

Put the mascarpone, milk, and sugar in a bowl and beat until smooth. Transfer the mixture to an ice cream machine and churn until almost frozen. Fold in the crumbled cookies and continue churning until the mixture is completely frozen. Transfer to a freezerproof container and freeze until ready to serve.

If you are making the ice cream without a machine, first freeze the mixture in a shallow container. When almost solid, beat it well with a wire whisk or electric beater until smooth, then return to the freezer. Repeat the process twice more to break down the ice crystals, folding in the crumbled cookies before returning it to the freezer for the final time. The result will be a smooth, silky ice cream.

Transfer to the refrigerator for 20–30 minutes before serving to soften. Best eaten within a week of being made.

Conversion chart

Weights and measures have been rounded up or down slightly to make measuring easier.

Measuring butter:

A US stick of butter weighs 4 oz. which is approximately 115 g or 8 tablespoons. The recipes in this book require the following conversions:

1 stick	115 g	4 oz.
7 tbsp	100 g	3½ oz.
6 tbsp	85 g	3 oz.

Weight equivalents:

Ounces	Grams
1 oz.	30 g
2 oz.	55 g
3 oz.	85 g
3½ oz	100g
4 oz.	115 g
5 oz.	140 g
6 oz.	175 g
7 oz.	200 g
8 oz. (½ lb.)	225 g
9 oz.	250 g
10 oz.	280 g
11½ oz.	325 g
12 oz.	350 g
13 oz.	375 g
14 oz.	400 g
15 oz.	425 g
16 oz. (1 lb.)	450 g
2 lb.	900 g

Oven temperatures:

150°C	(300°F)	Gas 2
160°C	(325°F)	Gas 3
180°C	(350°F)	Gas 4
190°C	(375°F)	Gas 5
200°C	(400°F)	Gas 6
220°C	(425°F)	Gas 7
230°C	(450°F)	Gas 8

Measurements:

Inches	Cm
¼ inch	5 mm
½ inch	1 cm
1 inch	2.5 cm
2 inches	5 cm
3 inches	7 cm
4 inches	10 cm
5 inches	12 cm
6 inches	15 cm
7 inches	18 cm
8 inches	20 cm
9 inches	23 cm
10 inches	25 cm

Volume equivalents:

American	Metric	Imperial
1 teaspoon	5 ml	
1 tablespoon	15 ml	
¼ cup	60 ml	2 fl.oz.
⅓ cup	75 ml	2½ fl.oz.
½ cup	125 ml	4 fl.oz.
⅔ cup	150 ml	5 fl.oz. (¼ pint)
¾ cup	175 ml	6 fl.oz.
1 cup	250 ml	8 fl.oz.

Credits
Recipes

Linda Collister: pages 10, 13, 14, 17, 18, 21, 24, 27, 28, 31, 32, 35, 36, 38, 40, 43, 44, 48, 59

Clare Ferguson: page 47

Liz Franklin: page 60

Hattie Ellis: page 52

Louise Pickford: page 56

Fran Warde: page 55

Photographs

Key: tr=top right, br=bottom right, tl=top left, bl=bottom left

Diana Miller: pages 1, 2, 4–5, 6, 8 tl, tr, & bl, 11, 12, 15, 19, 20, 22 tl & br, 26, 29, 30, 37, 38 tl, tr, & bl, 41, 42, 45, 49, 62

Martin Brigdale: pages 22 tr, 25, 34, 38 br, 46, 50 tr, 58

Patrice de Villiers: pages 8 br, 16, 22 bl, 33

Debi Treloar: pages 50 bl, 53, 54

William Lingwood: page 50 br, 61

Ian Wallace: page 50 tl, 57